VLARF

THE HUGH MacLENNAN POETRY SERIES

Editors: Allan Hepburn and Carolyn Smart

TITLES IN THE SERIES

Waterglass Jeffery Donaldson

All the God-Sized Fruit Shawna Lemay

Chess Pieces David Solway

Giving My Body to Science Rachel Rose

The Asparagus Feast S.P. Zitner

The Thin Smoke of the Heart Tim Bowling

What Really Matters Thomas O'Grady

A Dream of Sulphur Aurian Haller

Credo Carmine Starnino

Her Festival Clothes Mavis Jones

The Afterlife of Trees Brian Bartlett

Before We Had Words S.P. Zitner

Bamboo Church Ricardo Sternberg

Franklin's Passage David Solway

The Ishtar Gate Diana Brebner

Hurt Thyself Andrew Steinmetz

The Silver Palace Restaurant Mark Abley

Wet Apples, White Blood Naomi Guttman

Palilalia Jeffery Donaldson

Mosaic Orpheus Peter Dale Scott

Cast from Bells Suzanne Hancock

Blindfold John Mikhail Asfour

Particles Michael Penny

A Lovely Gutting Robin Durnford

The Little Yellow House Heather Simeney MacLeod

Wavelengths of Your Song Eleonore Schönmaier

But for Now Gordon Johnston

Some Dance Ricardo Sternberg
Outside, Inside Michael Penny
The Winter Count Dilys Leman
Tablature Bruce Whiteman
Trio Sarah Tolmie
hook nancy viva davis halifax
Where We Live John Reibetanz
The Unlit Path Behind the House Margo Wheaton
Small Fires Kelly Norah Drukker
Knots Edward Carson
The Rules of the Kingdom Julie Paul
Dust Blown Side of the Journey Eleonore Schönmaier
slow war Benjamin Hertwig
The Art of Dying Sarah Tolmie
Short Histories of Light Aidan Chafe
On High Neil Surkan
Translating Air Kath MacLean
The Night Chorus Harold Hoefle
Look Here Look Away Look Again Edward Carson
Delivering the News Thomas O'Grady
Grotesque Tenderness Daniel Cowper
Rail Miranda Pearson
Ganymede's Dog John Emil Vincent
The Danger Model Madelaine Caritas Longman
A Different Wolf Deborah-Anne Tunney
rushes from the river disappointment stephanie roberts
A House in Memory David Helwig
Side Effects May Include Strangers Dominik Parisien
Check Sarah Tolmie
The Milk of Amnesia Danielle Janess
Field Guide to the Lost Flower of Crete Eleonore
    Schönmaier
Unbound Gabrielle McIntire

Ripping down half the trees Evan J

whereabouts Edward Carson

The Tantramar Re-Vision Kevin Irie

Earth Words: Conversing with Three Sages John Reibetanz

Vlarf Jason Camlot

Vlarf

JASON CAMLOT

McGill-Queen's University Press
Montreal & Kingston • London • Chicago

ISBN 978-0-2280-0813-2 (paper)
ISBN 978-0-2280-0928-3 (ePDF)
ISBN 978-0-2280-0929-0 (ePUB)

Legal deposit third quarter 2021
Bibliothèque nationale du Québec

Printed in Canada on acid-free paper that is 100% ancient forest free
(100% post-consumer recycled), processed chlorine free

Funded by the Government of Canada   Financé par le gouvernement du Canada | Canadä   Canada Council for the Arts   Conseil des arts du Canada

We acknowledge the support of the Canada Council for the Arts.

Nous remercions le Conseil des arts du Canada de son soutien.

Library and Archives Canada Cataloguing in Publication

Title: Vlarf / Jason Camlot.

Names: Camlot, Jason, 1967– author.

Series: Hugh MacLennan poetry series.

Description: Series statement: The Hugh MacLennan poetry series |
Poems.

Identifiers: Canadiana (print) 20210244658 | Canadiana (ebook)
20210244682 | ISBN 9780228008132 (softcover) |
ISBN 9780228009283 (PDF) | ISBN 9780228009290 (EPUB)

Classification: LCC PS8555.A5238 V35 2021 | DDC C811/.6—dc23

This book was typeset by Marquis Interscript in 9.5/13 Sabon.

CONTENTS

Lost Days   3

Romantic Behaviour   4

Mr Hyde at Home (The Musical)   5

In the Criminal's Cabinet, Sherlock Holmes Discovers
   Himself   6

The Fruit Man   8

Men of Letters   20

Genealogy   21

The Leaf   22

Flowers   24

Stem   26

Root   28

Stones   29

Moss   32

Clouds   34

Lines Left   35

First and Last Stanzas From Poems Found in *The Worm's
   Kitchen: A Pantry of Light Verse for Dark Evenings*,
   Edited by Sir Jasper Evans Campbell   36

Why I Am Not a Modernist   45

Telempathus   49

Two Limericks   50

Queen Victoria   51

Animal Slippers   53

The Worms of Saint Peter's   58

Fudge in Entropy   59

Living Devices   74

Notes   75

Acknowledgments   79

For we other Victorianists,
the ones with whom we whom

The Victorian period is alive today.
The sandwich men are lurking in the streets.
They invented new machines for threshing wheat,
hammers for pummeling men back into clay,
systems to guarantee that workers pay
with lacerated hands and blistered feet.
Victorian children learned to cheat
properly, to apologize always
when battling other children to the death.
A was for Asylum, B for Bricks, C
for Crimean War. Victorian breath
was just like ours, but lacey.
Believe me,
when I say they prayed with words like "Saith."
Their deeds have lived on for an eternity.

On a shelf behind the first issue of the *Review of Closet Verse*
with some newly discovered letters by Joanna Baillie
(authoress of *Plays of the Passions*) to Lord Byron
(author of *Don Juan*), there is a finger device.

In each psychological year, you climb stairs
to the library, experience a *déjà vu*,
leaf through verbatim pages in a panic
(for the passage about what Manfred *really* means

when he says, "Oblivion – self-oblivion!")
and then slip your hand into the space between odd numbers,
prodding for the deadening vise. The same mercury pain travels
your skeleton until old numbness

relieves you of hope for change. Released then,
you tenderly return the volume, retreat
from the familiar pattern, and stand between parted curtains,
entwining fresh fingers into a horn for dull screams.

MR HYDE AT HOME (THE MUSICAL)

The knife-marks on the door
are not my own, they were there before.
I rent this Soho cabinet
with its primitive furnace and kitchenette.
I just want to be left alone
to my desires, to my own
habit of composing blasphemies
in the margins of my prophecies.
Let them – these dull phrenologists
and eager criminologists –
use their big words without apology.
I'll punch them right in their nosology,
and then retire here to drink tea,
and bite lips off China cups from the last Jubilee.
They seek me because I am obscure,
the unspeakable form behind the door.
They scar me with nomenclature:
atavistic blackguard troll,
bachelor, professional,
then run to their confessionals,
repenting for their little lusts.
My lusts are large, swollen, and round,
my taste is delicate and sound.
I'm happy just to stay at home,
smarten my beard with a pocket comb,
to stoke the fire,
and draw the wires
through eye-hole screws,
to catch up on the week's reviews,
to hang my pictures, summer scenes
with grasses green, heavens serene.

IN THE CRIMINAL'S CABINET, SHERLOCK
HOLMES DISCOVERS HIMSELF

Holmes entered the cabinet
of the respectable reverend
(who was in fact a closet naturalist)
and found so many Victorian things.

There were teapots
and rare fatal cannons,
coffins filled with roses,
and tinted canvases in frames.

Along one wall were hats on parade,
and fabrics apparently
from the time of Moses.
Behind one glass case could be seen

brass of superior quality,
and effigies of a more primitive culture.
Behind another:
artistic applications of electrotype,

snuffed tapers and chandeliers,
and beneath a glass table top,
instruments for the manipulation of teeth.
Holmes admired the Japanned goods.

He wondered at the strange colonial livestock,
and the new technology in underclothes.
Umbrellas opened and closed apathetically.
Then he found the full collection of thimbles.

These tiny monstrosities of lead
he screwed onto his fingertips
to help explore himself further
without fear of poisoned needles.

THE FRUIT MAN

Have done with sorrow;
I'll bring you plums tomorrow
Christina Rossetti, "*Goblin Market*"

Part I

Once a week his truck pulled up,
a blackened box on rusty wheels.
Ski-doo boots splayed
like size-ten banana peels,
overripe and lined with fleece,
he trudged on our pristine snow
crushing rinds and seeds
deep into the creases
of his treads,
his tracks, bas-reliefs
of a pomegranate's insides,
the late-fruit's aftermath,
in heavy pairs up our path.
My mother alone
in the paisley kitchen,
talking on the phone,
one of her sisters wishing
calamity upon
her other one
as far as I can tell,
from my little room upstairs.
Ten year old me,

Oscar Mellanby,
happy as a pea
in a single-windowed pod, only
with motifs of boats and the sea,
surrounding me,
and my imaginary
albatross, Alby.
My portal mirror on the wall
promises that I'll be tall
enough one day to travel all
the way from Montreal
to the summits of Nepal
and back again in time to keep
my mother from her deep despair.
My mother is my single care,
she travels with me everywhere
because I would not dare
leave her alone,
she being prone
to sadness, to sorrow,
to a lack of gladness.
It worries me incessantly,
or if not that,
then still a lot
for a ten-year-old
with an imaginary
albatross.
        He's invisible to all but me.
I see Alby easily,
an albatross of modest height,
his feather-cloak tight a bit
upon his paunchy seabird frame,
the girth a sign of his past fame

now come to roost as laziness,
self-satisfaction, and excess.
He ran with Charles Baudelaire
and Coleridge in his wilder days,
and sometimes he'll still share
an absinth, an anchovy pear,
a polonaise and a drunken haze
with the derelict birds downtown.
But mostly he just hangs around
my blue suburban bedroom,
gazing out the window at the Maple tree –
its solid branches and dancing leaves,
or icy twigs, as the case may be –
weaving tales of degenerate gloom,
and languishing in malaise.
He likes it here because of me –
ten year old Oscar Mellanby,
who understands melancholy –
and also because when The Fruit Man rings
(despite Alby's distrust
of the old man's claim
to eat fruit, exclusively)
he loves to hear the lists of things,
delicious fruits and savories,
like dimple-dotted-dew-berries
downy-dabbed ground cherries
purple-pop plums
and Senegal gum,
black pendulous grapes
with conical shapes,
apricot tape from the Barbary cape,
and the effervescent glory-sprouts
The Fruit Man loves to talk about.

"He comes," said Alby in a whisper,
and sure enough there was the truck,
and there the man with hunter's cap,
ears concealed by big ear flaps,
bulbous nose with wiry hairs
protruding from big nostrils flared,
his pockets filled, no doubt,
with fruits we strain to think about.
The doorbell rings and Alby swings
his podgy form onto my shoulder
as I tiptoe to the top of the stairs
from where we see my mother's hair
blown slightly by the winter air
that enters the house as she opens the door.
           "God bless the honest herbivore,"
was The Fruit Man's usual greeting.
his livelihood being in produce,
he took a stance against meat-eating.
(But as I've already said,
Alby felt this stance a sham,
and swore this merchant would eat ham,
and poultry, mutton, beef, and lamb.
He swore the peddler would easily trade
an apple, fig, peach, pear, or plum
for albatross sopped in a marinade.)
"Good day, old man," my mother said,
"it's good of you to come."
The Fruit Man bowed his head.
"What fruit do you have today?"
my mother asked, as Alby lay
in wait for the copious list
about to be heard.
"Beautiful fruit. Fresh, fresh, fresh.

Glistening, sparkling, crispy, the best!"
And then we waited
for The Fruit Man's list.
But the old man stood there,
shy and dumb.
"Bananas?" asked my mother,
"Do you have some?"
The Fruit Man looked glum.
He shook his head, "No bananas today,
I'm sorry to say."
Concerned my mother asked again,
what fruit The Fruit Man did have,
and the old man answered as before:
"I have beautiful fruit. Fresh, fresh, fresh.
Glistening, sparkling, crispy, the best!
"Well what, then?"
She grew impatient, The Fruit Man sensed.
He straightened up in self-defence
and gestured with knotty hands, to say
now was the time to dispense with all pretense.
"Today I have, special for you … "
(And finally Alby would get his list.
He had been working himself into such a tempest.
I was surprised my mom didn't notice
a ruffled albatross
in a huff at the top of the stairs.
But then again, to see the imagination
of someone you love more than yourself
can be frightening, and is rare,
even when it's noisy, big, and everywhere.)
" … Baldwins, Mutsus,
Northern Spies,
Boskoops, Crispins

Benoni,
Arkansas Blacks and Dapplegaps,
Black Gilliflowers, and Imperial Blues,
Cox Orange Pippins and Magdelaines,
I have three prismatic Criterions,
McIntoshes, Yorks, and one Red Champlain.
I'll bring out a basket and you can choose."
But my mother stood confused.
And as The Fruit Man made his way
back to his truck, the dismay
I saw on my mother's face
held me quietly in my place
"It's a disgrace," she said,
in reference to the old man's speech,
although precisely what it was he said
to make me fear to tread
around her mood,
I would not have understood,
if Alby hadn't spoken next:
"Dapplegaps!" He relished in the word
with the fierce pleasure
of a raptorial bird.
"There's no such apple as a Dapple!"
he announced as much to hear
the sound as to volunteer
the fact.
And then I understood.
The Fruit Man didn't have
the stock of fruits he should.
He had apples. No other fruit,
and lacked any sense of shame to boot
(at least, that was my mother's claim).
Before the old man could knock again

(he returned with a basket full to the brim
of apples that all looked much the same)
my mother said, "Nothing today!"
and sent The Fruit Man on his way.
She stood with her back
to the hard, fastened door
as we listened to the pleading,
begging, pounding, whining,
pelting, thumping, kicking, and crying
hurled like a tempest from the other side,
and waited for the tantrum to subside.
When it did and silence reigned,
she opened the door again,
wishing, I think, that the gnarled old man
might still be in sight to invite back in.
But The Fruit Man left without a trace,
except for one green apple
placed in the snow, now at her feet,
on our front step.
One little green apple
left there for free.
She put it alone in a big glass bowl,
a lonely apple without its tree.
This is something we must not eat,
she made herself clear to me.

Part II

In Alby's talons I felt safe
despite my fear of heights
and some discomfort
at the nape of my neck.

I was amazed to see
my little house in mist and snow,
my icy leafless maple tree,
a tiny dream of home
fathoms of cold below me
as we flew
through the night
above suburban forests
and dim-lit fields,
and soon above a city
sparkling with lights
like emeralds and ice.
I held on tightly
to the apple in my hand,
the fruit we hoped would lead us
to the man behind
my mother's sadness.
And as we traveled through the sky
I saw my mother cry
as she had cried relentlessly
since The Fruit Man had gone away.
I saw so many wondrous things
that I had only imagined.
Alby had intimations
we followed resolutely.
His inklings always led to places
I had never been,
to feelings I had never felt
and sights I'd never seen.

        First, a blue and gold basilica
with kneeling worshippers
who wore red robes and sang dark songs,
and kept a log of all their doubts,

anxieties and wrongs,
and carried orange candles in their mouths.
When Alby asked them if they knew
The Fruit Man, whether he'd passed through
their sanctuary recently,
one worshipper ceased chewing,
singing, doubting and explained,
"Not fruit but candles do we eat,
and sweet angelica."
                And then we searched through Chinatown
as curious snowflakes floated down.
I saw five plucked ducks hung in a row,
necks stretched long and featherless flesh
purple and blue as a sailor's sunset.
Two big pigs with bullet wound noses
and triangle ears curled at the tips.
Open hands at the end of sticks
in barrels, and satin slippers with flat
white soles. Huge porcelain kittens,
peaceful and fat
as Caucasian heads
with plates of sweets
and slices of orange at their feet.
A gorgeous spectacle
of lucid color and animal meat.
"Ducks are so compliant. Stupid
ducks," Alby declared,
as he pinched my neck to move along,
and dusted the snow
from his outstretched wings
Then in the vast brick buildings
of Alexander Street,
long plank corridors

led us to a factory hall
with blinded windows
along one wall
and shattered doors
like tablets strewn
in one obscure corner,
and unshaded bulbs at rest on strings
descending from dust-coated beams,
and without a floor,
but an uncanny trembling sea
of animal hair breaking like waves
in tufts and woolly mammoth curls,
against my knees.
I waded in to see
what a hundred workers
were making in their factory.
"A sable coat for a behemoth,"
one worker whispered as he passed.
When I asked the foreman if he'd seen
a fruit man selling apples, green,
like this one in my hand,
he brought me to his cabinet
of cardboard drawers
filled with buttons and safety pins,
butcher's paper, razor blades,
and numberless scraps of animal skin.
In a pantry for needles,
behind a sewing machine,
is where the foreman kept his apples,
green, like the one in my hand,
brought weekly to him
by the same Fruit Man.
The foreman told us where to go.

North, to the ghetto,
where the houses were dark,
and dirt lightly covered
half-melted snow.
Up a narrow flight of stairs
misshapen by oppressive air,
closed in by walls with trivial light.
As we climbed we saw a girl
laughing wildly without sound.
We moved towards an attic room
heavily on steep, distorted steps.
We were not even halfway up
when suddenly the battered door
was opened wide and at the top
with a stoic bow
The Fruit Man said we had arrived.
        As we crossed
into The Fruit Man's home
the laughing girl reappeared
and with her neck stretched long
called out from far below
words we could not hear.
The Fruit Man grinned
and whirled around.
He sat us in his bright kitchen,
gave us tea, and hardly
ever taking his eyes off me,
with a silver, pointed spoon
took up a lump of sugar in his teeth
and sipped quietly from a porcelain cup
until his tea was all consumed.
"I have known your mother since she was a child.
She was prone to sadness then as now."

He swallowed his last sugar, smiled,
and said, "Her sadness is not your sadness,
and anyhow, she loves you without fail
through her necessary wars and trials
with whatever grief that burdens her."
Then he took the green apple
three weeks old but fresh as ever
from my hand, dug the point
of his tea spoon in, and split
the hard green fruit in half.
One pitch black seed, that's
all there was at the apple's core.
"What else does an apple need?
You wanted more?" The Fruit Man
asked. He held the seed
devoid of light
like the eye of a still child,
like undiluted hopelessness,
like a tear for chaos, shame and loss,
like a bead of sorrow's endlessness
in his impervious, gnarled hand.

He lodged the black seed in my side.

In 1826 John Stuart Mill suffered
his first mental crisis. He saw the aim of his desires
but he did not desire the aim of his desires.
He understood that he no longer felt.

Upon reading the *Mémoires* of Marmontel
(and a passage about the death of that author's father,
in particular) John Stuart wept consistently until
the early 1830s, when he first became a man

of letters. In a monthly repository he stored
ideas about the intuitive truth of some words.
His father had raised him as an experiment
in education, and had taught him the uselessness

of wild imagination. But John Stuart, with all
due respect, felt that words should be used
to tear through the lucid veil as well as
to teach what is pushpin.

Years later, long after his father was dead,
John Stuart suffered his second mental
crisis, which he passed over in silence. He posed
for a portrait showing the fragile head

with its many bumps, signs of wisdom,
or perhaps heartbreak. Another important Victorian
thinker, John Ruskin, did not speak for the last
twelve years of his life, although his collected

works fill many thousands of pages.

GENEALOGY

Between "dear" and "drear" or "pear" and "spear"
there is excellent dissonance,
war proving connection.

Similarly, the crisp final 'k' in such specimens
as the "broken thing" or the "beggar's rag"
proves them all from the same monstrous tribe.

At present I work on the origins of the orange lily,
with its shadows of half-purple fur,
and the obscure quality of its cloven device.

It is found but rarely in narrow arbitrary localities.
I have noticed how it shuns the light,
and those I have brought home to keep

in water respond as if burnt by darkness,
crumbling fast into crystal fibres clear as dew
and more dismal than hoar-frost.

So, I possess no specimens of the orange lilies.
Nor do I know where they have come from. But surely
they are the most beautiful creatures in the world.

THE LEAF

It will be helpful to consider every
        leaf
as a separate portion
to be sung.

We possess some facts:
The greenish-black ones are like a tree's turtles.
There is the fact of dew; and in the center
rib or spine are veins.

This said, much is still unknown.
The division of the breeze by the leaf petal
gives but a faint image of how the wind felt.
Also, there is the mystery of "green leaf."

From a sentimental angle we can observe
how some people collect them as keepsakes,
like dried confessions, and how our love
of the leaf is shown in tracery.

Their physical properties are surprising:
Though airy in handfuls,
there is much weight within
a single leaf held by its stem.

They keep well in winter,
and sometimes like jagged mouths
they appear
frozen in the lake ice.

And then they suffocate in shallow pits,
are digested with wood,
and transform
into charcoal and muck.

My botanical book speaks
of exogenous stems
plunged into lead.
I don't in the least want to know what this means.

I prefer to understand them
as the ground's trembling scales,
the soil thus sung
in choral shiver.

FLOWERS

The flower's death is an offering,
like dust falling
into zones of fire.

In summer we come upon the gifts
of bracts and stalks and tori and calices and
corollas and discs and stamens and pistils.

Take that cluster of bog-heather bells.
Bunch them into a star.
They can only be drawn as they grow.

Take the dark contortion, the pale
wasting, the quiet closing of
the brown bells of the ling.

Take this foretaste of faerie-
flowers, their petals wavering
like the wings of human moths.

Take this tiny red poppy,
all silk and flame, burning
in its own scarlet cup.

If you offer a small bouquet
of four, one pair is always
smaller than the other.

Take this humble host
of green syllables familiarly
Englished into nectar!

Take them from me gently,
and then cast the severed
leaves away.

One never thinks
of the stalk.
For instance,
grape-stalks with no grapes:
the little feet
like an animal's feet
hooking without
fruit.
Every living
ripple or jag
grows wild
upon a stem.
The profile
of the letter
I
resembles
a human shoot
from very far
away.
And deep in the 586th page
we find the Yew
Tree etymology,
the roots reaching
up inside the trunk
for lost vowels.

And don't you
ever wonder,
"If I were
a Tree?"
Quite right.
The growth of sadness
is patient work:
a dead
sorrow ever
insoluble
in a living one,
a rosary with
but one berry.
Using alike
our lips
and brains
we try to
understand
our words,
our trees,
our words for trees.
The wonder of it!

And not just that.
Look,
here is a little
thing:
the germ
curls.

ROOT

The part that loves the light is called the Leaf.
The Root, however, proves us fettered.

Subsequently we wonder
what it might mean

not to be a crawling thing,
and yet to be a crawling thing.

We look to the ground and see
plants moving like lizards,

and we conclude:
Root is a form of fate

contriving, writhing, coiling
to avoid any obstacle,

to split the rocks
and bind the rocks,

to grasp
the jagged edge.

August 1846:
Pudding stones.

August 1849:
A dream of revolutionary
ornament.

August 1853:
I have identified the nugatory as the third form
of true expression in work.
I am impatient to share this idea.

August 1867:
Flint-infused paste
divided into fragments by violence
and dried into tracts of iron-oxide.

August 1869:
I have marked the zones required
for inspired instruction
in the art of jewelry.
They are:
the zone of twisted fibres, the zone of ochre dust, the zone of
     accidental fibres,
the zone of enraptured ore, the zone of ruptured servitude, the
     zone of copper,
the zone of crystalline power, the zone of free play, and the
     zone of moral law.

August 1871:
With this ivory finger
one can make
animal art
according to my profane
tracts of how
stones can be jewels.

August 1873:
Stars of flint are first deadly
instead of useful.

August 1874:
A dream:
the crystallization of miracles.

August 1881:
The sapphires order into ranks
and battalions
but thankfully leave my books
un-pierced.
(Do they spare my work out of gratitude?)

August 1886:
I have here in my hand
crags of flint jelly,
some of excellent precision.
I will store them so they may be visited deep
in the choke-cavities of my old glass house,
where once shame teemed
like the guilt and rain
of people.

August 1887:
What is to become of the silversmiths?

August 1899:
If they are still confused
by the nervous power of the eye,
let them focus on the brain-opal.
This will renew their faith
in the veins of social affection.

More, I cannot advise.

MOSS

I observe a plant
growing on other plants
in dense festoons.

Thin red threads
sleeping on the heads
of wheat.

Tiny
forests of little
brown stems.

A crest of spears
balancing
an emerald.

I
see,
barely.

This is the way
mosses leave die:
they decay invisibly

in continual
secession
beneath the crest.

I do not doubt
that we carry
memories of moss.

If you have walked
moorlands enough
you will have felt them.

So much for the human
meaning
of that decay.

I must beg
your pardon that
I do not assert.

I merely wander unshod,
shedding hope
in guarded fields,

my living feet
alive
to all the dying threads.

CLOUDS

Every cloud is definable against our own horrible acts.

Today I remark,
high in the air
and nearly motionless
the bars of cloud,
green,
the bars of sky-green
and *green*
in the sunset at Abbeville, 1868.

LINES LEFT

I had a string
of futile-feelings
about the dabchicks.
But no longer.

Blue Little Song

The little blue book chirps and swallows
like a rhasper in the hollows.

...
...
...
...
...

But, of course, this promise earns
only hungry moths and worms.

My Blood Carpet

I let the blood
            into the parlour
curious to see
            if it would run farther.

…
…

And when my love pulls his feet in
            I feel a great pang to eat him,
as if he's come fresh from the market
            to this plate, my blood carpet.

Our Noctambulones

They say that our noctambulones,
our drones who travel in their sleep,
blow somnambulistic trombones
for our dreaming children's souls to keep.

...
...

O sleep and travel in your sleep.
Sleep in blue regalia.
And pray that those who do not sleep
are too frightened to betray ya.

Paper Pill

The exotic organ music
made a bloody mess of Elgin.

...
...
...

"We run rabid with the organ music playing."

Royal Snack

Lord Lord
with the green shrimp dangling
from the corner of his mouth.

…
…
…

Gored Gored
albeit chewed, not beaten
plucked from the deep where its green love lies.

T

I fed the language monster
and he spat me up a word.

…
…

I thanked the creature anyhow
and gave him more to feed on,
and once we'd swallowed tea and eels,
then we sailed away to *Ceylon*.

Tassels

He's about to go in,
He's about to sit down,
then he'll tackle the great English canon.

…
…
…
…

For you know the next day
when it comes time to pay
The Librarians will come a-reaping.

The Creeps

The Creeps are in the bedroom
and they're donning satin aprons.

...

...

...

...

...

...

...

He'll found a sheer museum
filled with frilly waxwork creatures.

The Locust Piles

The Halloween Beetles
live in orange caves
and impale on sharp nettles
their dull locust slaves.

...
...
...
...

Here a most famous Beetle,
who survived classification
frees scutellum from needle
to the crowd's clicking elation.

I am not a Modernist, I am a Victorianist.
Why? I think I would rather be
a Modernist, but I am not. Well,

for instance, Hugh Kenner
is starting an essay. I drop in.
"Sit down and have a spot of tea" he
says. I sip; we sip. I look
down. "You have MODERNISM in it."
"Oh." I go and the days go by
and I drop in again. The essay
is going on, and I go, and the days
go by. I drop in. The essay is
finished. "Where's MODERNISM?"
All that's left is just
dashes and blank space,
"It was too much," Hugh says.

But me? One day I am thinking of
a colour: eggshell. I write a book
about eggshell. Pretty soon it is a
multivolume work, not just a few books.
Then another multivolume work.
There should be
so much more, not of eggshell,
of eggs, of how terrible shells are,
and of the yoke of poverty.
Years go by. It is even appearing
in serialized periodical form.

I am a real Victorianist. My
multivolume work
is finished and I haven't mentioned
sexual intercourse yet.
It's thirty-nine volumes, I call
it *The Queen of Autumn's Sepulcher:*
A Study of Inscrutable Codicils,
with Official Tables Appended,
Summarizing the Report
of the Select Committee
on the Ten-Hour
Factory Bill, Vindicated
in a Series of Letters
Addressed to John Elliot
Henry William
Percival Flatelle, Esquire,
One of the Factory
Commissioners,
Rebutted in a Series
of Pointed Responses, Composed
in Anagrammatic Verse, by the Reverend
Reginald Winsome, with
Accompanying Charts,
in Colour, Depicting the Condition
of Faith in Workers Who Have
Not Been Subjected
to Factory Education,
Annotated by Elliot John
Edward Charles William
Henry Drylock, MP,
with Insights Upon Factory
Education, its Extension,
and on the Practicability

of its Application to Other
Trades and Occupations,
such as Potting,
Slate Quarrying,
Copse-Cutting,
Butty Ganging,
Mudlarking,
Rat Catching,
Sawyering, Shepherding,
Tin Mining, Dressmaking,
Slopping, Gardening,
and Polling the Willow,
with Entertaining Stories
Enlivening the Annotations
Selected from Chapters
in the Life, and Other Gay
Romps of Experience,
of a Dundee Factory
Lad (An Autobiography),
with Humorous Engravings
of Curious Factory Lad Exploits
as Interpreted by Joseph
Henry William William
K. Claringbull, Renowned Engraver
of Twelve Crochet Edgings,
with Illustrative Engravings, *Edited*
By Henry John William Edgar
G. Curling Hope, author of The Art
of Crochet *and* My Working Friend,
Embellished with Crochet Patterns,
Including Luna, Narva,
Lola Montes, and L'Infanta Lace,
Dentelle Passementerie,

Wheatsheaf Pattern, and Leaf Edging,
Derived from The Knitter's Friend;
Being a Selection of Receipts
for the Most Useful and Saleable
Articles in Knitting, Netting,
and Crochet Work, *as well*
as from Madame Goubaud's
Crochet Book, *Lightly Embossed*
in Soft Lactescent Paper, Along
the Edges of the Most Engrossing
Pages, as Selected by The Author.

And one day in a little magazine
I see Hugh's essay, called MODERNISM.

Telemachus means far away fighter.

Telempathus is a lesser-known son.

Lesser known to those and they and them.

He lives asleep through all their greatest fears.

He, conventionally, has no self-control.

Telempathus surges the sorrow *live*.

No cartoon panel illustrates his dreams.

He cannot miss a single nighttime death.

He does not think his empathy an art.

Telempathus just wants a good night's sleep.

His critics praise dramas of exhaustion.

There may be art in knowing how screams feel.

There may be art in tasting someone's fear.

The empathizee's pain is not a trap.

Telempathus is too polite to cry.

Telempathus mutters as someone else.

New flocks of coffins find him every night.

They bring vicarious sleep and sudden dreams.

Telempathus sips dolphin's milk from shells.

He bites into the pearls of life like gum.

He grips their goblets with his scalded hands.

Anoints himself in lamentation.

Sees sullen people wave hello goodbye.

Writes urgent postcards with quivering eyelids.

You are not missing from Telempathus.

His dream is to retreat, but not to dream.

TWO LIMERICKS

I. Limerick of 1837

An Earl in 1837
Feared he would not get to heaven,
For when he counted his sins
There were the five sets of twins,
Plus The Lump, which adds up to eleven.

II. Limerick of the Sea

There was a mate from Aberystwyth,
A wrench his skiff he liked to twist with.
He tightened in front
'Till they'd let out a grunt,
Then a rag the tool he wiped forthwith with.

Queen Victoria,
your tobacco
forms
a German
pink
prince in me.

Queen Victoria,
all your cold
dirty
empty
ornaments
are gone.

Queen Victoria,
your lace
bibles drown
in mechanical
musty
bidets.

Queen Victoria,
you nursed me
upon
sorrow-
perfect
memorials.

Queen Victoria,
your century
giants
have tested
every
heavy
star-dazed
loss.

ANIMAL SLIPPERS

Book I

this is my
marker

the
marker
defies

the
two
hermits

ornaments
for
gravestones

water
level

this
sudden
boundary

a birth
mark

the
dead

how
to
play

we
are
not
people

Book II

fading
fading

glad

an
archival
researcher

the mental
surface

scudding
and
pouncing

points
and
lines

55

the sign post

There must be one more story to tell before this book ends. A spot on the surface of the earth that will establish a sign post by which others may determine a sense of direction

When Oscar Wilde made me tea that time he trod laboriously across the linoleum floor of his simple kitchen to set the water a-boil in an open tin pot. He wore furry slippers with calf-skin soles. He dropped the tea right in the pot, stirred it around a bit and then used a tea towel to filter the leaves from the liquid he poured into two mismatched cups

animal slippers

It made quite a mess and the tea towel was stained an unfortunate brownish yellow. We sat in two worn armchairs around the wobbly tea table. The tea was served black.

black tea

He had brought an open box of stale tea biscuits to the table and now we dipped them into our dark bitter tea and nibbled and sipped silently for the next ten minutes. Finally, he wiped his chin.

dark bitter tea

I asked him how he could propose a scale of uselessness as a theory of aesthetic evaluation and he replied. I asked him why he did not surround himself with beautiful things in his own home and he replied. I changed the subject to nature.

he replied

I told him I had allergies to grass, trees, ragweed, and to dust mites. We returned to our tea and biscuits for about ten minutes in silence.

nature

Then we turned on the television and watched situations. We played some lame personal shooter game that he had, I did not understand. A spider wove a web in a corner above the TV set. The telephone rang. Oscar Wilde was offered a cooking show but turned it down.

a spider

I asked Oscar Wilde if he thought some people were better than other people. Oscar Wilde asked me to pass the biscuits. There had been a sale on chunk white tuna at the grocery store today, two cans for the price of one and a half cans. He had bought six cans.

*six
cans*

*drama for
children*

Oscar Wilde composed now primarily by humming. He has a new play for young animals coming out this winter.

Oscar Wilde has eaten sunflowers in Paris. Or, was it cornflowers. He wasn't sure. I asked Oscar Wilde if he was recording this conversation and he replied. I asked him a series of either/or questions: Tea or Coffee. Pen or Pencil. Love or *Love*.

*either
or*

*we
carried
on*

Poetry or *Poetry*. Sometimes he replied yes or no. We went on like this for many years, and then Oscar Wilde made us some more tea to drink. We were out of biscuits.

*towards
an end*

THE WORMS OF SAINT PETER'S

The worms of Saint Peter's
are stuck in the heaters
they're mooers, not bleaters
some are seven feeters
while others, like cheaters
hook up by their ridges
and construct wormy bridges.

Ten thousand hearts pounding
are not heard resounding
which is rather confounding
but far less astounding
than the two local groundlings
who cause thunder while eating
and brimstone when breeding.

I. Lines Crossed Out II

Hi, I'm Fudge, a guinea pig.

As if you couldn't tell.

Not long haired, just regular haired.

How did you get here?

Do you like Nava's room?

I like it.

But it has gotten a bit lonely.

Are you shy?

Anyhow.

This little blank notebook I'm nibbling on was originally given to Dad my owner by the Painter when he went to visit her in her studio sometime back in the 1990s.

It's very small for a human notebook, like the size of my food bowl, only not heart-shaped but rectangular. Black-wrapped cardboard cover with red corners; lined pages inside. Made in China, I think. Cheap. But small, which was the reason for the little gift.

She gave it to him to prove a point about the impact of scale upon artistic process.

In this case, the impact of the size of Dad's medium – paper sheet, notebook – on how he was using words.

My Dad-owner is a poet.

In that dream he brought the Painter poems to read – to look at.

The Painter showed Dad what she thought of the poems.

She didn't read them as he would have expected.

She didn't read them for meaning.

She read them as lists of words and phrases, some powerful, others distracting.

She worked on the words by taking a sheet of tracing paper, covering his poems and crossing out all of his words that got in the way of the emotion she was seeking.

She felt that some words could get in the way, crowd out the potency of other more powerful words and phrases.

These words are too crowded, she said, looking at one of his verbose pieces.

There is deadly overcrowding, she said.

She didn't say much more, but then she engaged with the words in front of him, crossing some out to free the others to breathe, she said.

It was a vivid gesture.

She didn't *explain* what she was doing, but he could see her interact with certain words and he could see the results of her annihilation.

The Painter crossed out whole words, whole lines, whole pages. It was like, whoa.

The rationale of her crossing-out was legible in small quivers around her eyes and mouth.

The quivers stood in for any explanation she might have provided in words.

My own opinion is, the quivers were the effect of energy newly released from the words she had transformed by murdering other adjacent ones.

My owner Dad the poet saw what she was doing and he understood it meant that his poems could no longer mean as he had intended them to mean.

His poems once were too crowded. Now that had to stop.

The Painter would make it stop.

The overcrowding in his poems was not fatal to people, or to other creatures, thanks be to god. Amen.

Yes, I'm Jewish. Yes, there are Jewish guinea pigs. There are more of us than you might think. No, I don't look Jewish. (I get that a lot.). But really, what does a Jewish guinea pig look like? I'm not orthodox or anything. But I identify. I'm sort of an atheist, but I identify with my Jewishness culturally.

You don't want to know what they sometimes do to guinea pigs.

No, you really don't want to know.

I'm very privileged.

I can sit here with a fresh green bean in my hands and talk to you about art and poetry.

I know all this stuff because my poet sometimes sleeps in my room and I can hear him dream.

And I remember.

On that visit, after the Painter showed Dad the lines crossed out, she gave him this tiny little book. Make your own poems with less words, she was saying. A poem should be able to fit onto one of these tiny book pages. You should be able to make a poem with just a few perfectly charged words. Ideally, your poems will have no words at all.

The Painter seemed to be saying all this when she gave him the cheap little book.

He never did use it for writing.

It fell from his night table onto the floor, and then Finnick took it under the bed for a few years, chewed it up a bit. Mom found it and plopped it in here just the other day. Something for me to do, I guess.

It's funny how the poems my owner made from the Painter crossing things out were eventually presented to her in an elaborately assembled artist's book, and how the poems – dense little stones of affect – were dead to her because the design of the book itself was too distractingly busy. Too materially verbose, so to speak. The book that held these remains of the Painter's crossings out involved thread and rope and wood and overly thin Japanese paper and punctures, and weavings, and some kind of elaborate pulley system, or something like that.

It was technologically clear in the dream. It's more cinematically vivid (than technically accurate) in memory.

It really was *chaloshes*, though. Garish, I believe, is the correct word for it.

Dad understood what the Painter meant by the subtle disgust on her face as she flipped the much-garnished book's pages, but, at the same time, he *thought* the book, overwrought with stitchery and an elaborate binding structure that required the pages to unfold in a perplexing way – was beautiful.

It was made by Dad-poet's friend, the Bookbinder. A fellow he respected and loved, and in whose apartment he was renting a room back then.

Dad understood what the Painter meant when she said the book's distractions neutralized whatever charge had been gained by pruning the poems into conductors of feeling.

The Painter was strong – violent – in the confidence of her opinions.

She *knew* that the book was over-crowded. She knew why the newly distilled, nearly vaporized poems were ineffective in this book of ruffles, eyelets and gears.

Out of sympathy and love for his friend the Bookbinder, Dad tried to assert a counter argument to this confident knowledge of hers – but the best that he could do was to think, not to know.

He thought it was beautiful.

He knew that it was not beautiful. He knew that it was *chaloshes*, to be honest.

Sometimes I think means I know but I wish I did not know that this certainty that I know is really true.

II. Blaze

Take the occasion of Blaze's death, for example. Blaze was a guinea pig who once lived in this overlarge cage with me in Nava's room – this room. Our room. Blaze was my brother.

Nava is my poet's eleven-year-old daughter.

Blaze was orange with a white racing stripe.

I am the color of chocolate and caramel fudge, clearly.

Hence our names.

Blaze was the shy and suspicious one.

I'm vocal, curious, but also laid back.

Blaze startled easily and was quick as a dart.

I'm more like, "I'm a-coming … "

We were Fudge and Blaze.

We would scurry and fight in the woodchips from time to time, as same sex sibling guinea pigs are wont to do, but never with harmful consequences.

We were loving.

Our fighting – like everything else we did in our world – was adorable to Nava, Dad-poet, Oscar-son, and Mom-Cory.

They were genuinely happy to have us. To them, it was like having two silky soft eggplants, two little soft-haired Winston Churchills living in our own self-sufficient, chippy pasture, on a desk in a young girl's room, emitting socially motivated R 2 D 2 sounds, crunching carrots and string beans, my brother Blaze in the cave, and me, Fudge, out in the open.

Do you like guinea pigs?

I like the way your eyes are round and flat.

Does your mouth ever open?

I'm sorry, you don't have to answer that.

My owner was on his way to the gym when Nava approached him quietly in distress.

"Can you come here?"

She asked him to come here, to the threshold of our little room.

"What is it?"

"I think," she said, "I think Blaze is dead."

She said she thought Blaze was dead and she wanted my owner to go and look into our cage.

His daughter Nava said she thought Blaze was dead, but really we knew Blaze was dead.

Sometimes, "I think, Blaze is dead" means "Blaze is dead."

He really was dead.

They had inherited me and Blaze from Nava's elementary school friend because her friend was moving back to Australia.

At the time, Blaze and I were residing in a decent cage set up in the Australians' basement laundry room.

The friend's father was in Montreal for a year for work and he bought us for his daughter, I can't recall her name, from a pet store.

Me and the Blazer were the first ones picked from the batch.

What was that Australian guy thinking? Right?

Did he not know that the typical life span of a guinea pig easily exceeds twelve months by at least four-to-five years, god willing?

Probably he knew and he was thinking in the moment of his family's arrival in a strange land that the acquisition of a Fudge and a Blaze would accelerate the transition of their rented semi-detached lower condo into a cozy home.

We can have that effect, because we pretty much ignore the big picture and go about our business like nothing is terribly wrong. We chew a lot.

We seem so earnest it's cute.

It's reassuring to people.

I suppose he was right – Nava's school acquaintance was a bit sad to part with us – but not so sad as to protest with a hunger strike or a disturbing fit of any kind.

She was excited to return home to Australia, to the dingoes and kangaroos and other creatures whose cuteness was linguistically enhanced by o-sounds, and even to those creatures whose names did not have such preposterous o-sounds.

She got over us, I guess. And so, I don't bother remembering her name.

That father knew what he was doing. He probably knew that *his* daughter would never have to know the fact of death, our inevitable death, the death of Fudge and Blaze.

Nava and I witnessed Blaze experience a violent seizure, heard as an erratic rattling of plastic from within the cave.

And then we saw Blaze lie still and unbreathing on his back, pink mouth wide open, beautiful little limbs and tiny humany hands unnaturally rigid.

We both knew Blaze was dead – but Nava used the discursive trick – the trick of "I think" – to extend his life ever so slightly, until Dad entered our room, looked into the cage, observed the rigidly demented form of Blaze, half in, half out of the cave and said, "Yes, Blaze is dead."

Only then – with the corroboration of her father upon the death of Blaze – did she transition to an uncontrollable fit of sobbing and anguish for four to five minutes.

I sat in the corner and nibbled on fresh green hay Dad had added in a big handful after he removed Blaze. I was kind of in shock.

It's hard to tell where you're looking, exactly. You seem to be focused on my breathing as much as my words.

Yes, things are slowing down.

I think I am delaying the inevitable.

Poor Blaze most probably did not know what he was experiencing when he was in the process of dying.

He did not know what was going on, in the Cartesian sense.

Consciousness clings to the knowledge of our existence as wood chips will inevitably cling to the coat of a guinea pig, even a regular-haired one.

I doubt Blaze could have realized.

At least, I hope not.

The scale of Blaze's life was quite different from the scale of my owner's life, or of his daughter's life, or of yours, I imagine.

III. Haika and Finnick

We get so tired at the end of a long story and we just want it to end.

I must admit, I'm feeling pretty weary.

But really, we wish it could go on forever.

So, recently, my owner sat in the bleachers of the park where he sometimes used to bring me and Blaze to graze in the summer, and he didn't know who he was.

He was reading *Bells and Pomegranates*.

Feisty Haika (a Terrier mix) and friendly-yet-confused Finnick (a Husky, Lab, Shih Tzu, and Bichon Frise mix) lay dramatically resigned on the ground in front of him.

(Haika and Finnick were endlessly interested in us. They'd stick their noses through the bars to sniff. It always scared the poop out of Blaze. Haika said our poop tasted like raisin Glosettes. Coming to see us was like going to the movies! Haika said this once in her quick, enthusiastic way. I was confident they knew not to eat us. Blaze wasn't so sure.)

Suddenly Dad stood up from the park bench and said a prayer in a mixture of Hebrew and English for his Auntie Irene who was going in for an operation.

Haika and Finnick stood up, alert to possibilities.

Baruch Atah Adonai
please let everything go
as it should
for her body
and her mind.

Bvakashah,
let her live
for as long
as she can
imagine living,
and as long
as we need her to live.

He sat down and returned to *Bells and Pomegranates*.

And then he got up again and continued his walk with Haika and Finnick.

As they walked he self-consciously addressed someone. I'm still not sure whom, exactly. And that's all I know.

I know this much because he slept in Nava's room again last night due to his snoring, and while he dreamed I felt everything he thought and said when he was taking the dogs out for their walk.

The snoring doesn't bother me.

I'm pretty nocturnal.

And I have enjoyed the company, since Blaze has passed.

Nava sleeps really silently, and I can't seem to hear her dream, for some reason.

I hear him loud and clear.

I can still feel the final speech of the poet's dream as I listened to him last night.

It feels like a prayer whispered to me as I rest:

O, you, whom I am addressing.

I have two white animals
tethered to my wrists
and they are leading me
around and around
the oval green.

They are so enthusiastic
in their intent to learn
more about the inhabitants
of our path.

I love them for it truly
even though they don't
always hear me, and
only sometimes listen.

I could pull them wherever
I wish, in truth.
But tonight, I am content
to trace the course
around and around

according to their pure
will
for life,
for feeling
life.

And where
it stops, nobody
knows.

LIVING DEVICES

I believe that somewhere
I have already observed
creatures tenderly bound.

I can't as yet find out.
Meanwhile I will look at them
and see the mystery of distance.

But how did they die?
is the first thing
I want to know about them.

Take this sandy vase
with its foretaste
of deathflowers

and the tracery
of human
bats.

And then at last
with my own broken
memories of snakes

I will hope
for the harvest, and coals
on my head.

Wikipedia explains that "Flarf poetry was an avant-garde poetry movement of the early 21st century. Its first practitioners, working in loose collaboration on an email listserv, used an approach that rejected conventional standards of quality and explored subject matter and tonality not typically considered appropriate for poetry. One of their central methods … was to mine the Internet with odd search terms then distill the results into often hilarious and sometimes disturbing poems, plays and other texts."

Vlarf refers to a form of Victorianist Flarf in which expressions of sentiment that may have become unfamiliar, unacceptable, uncool, since modernism, are pursued by mining Victorian texts and generic forms with odd inclinations, using techniques that include: erasure, cut up, *bout-rimé*, emulation, adaptation, reboot, mimicry, abhorrence, cringe, and love.

"Lost Days" is a *bout-rimé* poem based on the 1862 sonnet of the same title by D.G. Rossetti.

"Romantic Behaviour" makes reference to and is inspired in sentiment by Lord Byron's *Manfred: A Dramatic Poem* (1817).

"Mr Hyde at Home (The Musical)" is an imagined show tune sung from the perspective of Hyde wishing for the solitary domesticity of Jekyll's situation, based on Robert Louis Stevenson's *The Strange Case of Dr Jekyll and Mr Hyde* (1886). The poem was written in ignorance of Frank Widhorn's Broadway musical horror drama, *Jekyll & Hyde* (1997), and its more recent revivals.

"The Fruit Man" emulates aspects of Christina Rossetti's great work, *Goblin Market and Other Poems* (1862), combined with threads of my own Eastern European Yiddish family folklore.

"In the Criminal's Cabinet, Sherlock Holmes Discovers Himself" was inspired by the Holmes of Arthur Conan Doyle's *A Study in Scarlet* (1887) and later Holmes stories.

"Men of Letters" draws from the autobiographies of John Stuart Mill and John Ruskin, *Autobiography* (1873) and *Praeterita* (1886), respectively.

"Genealogy," "The Leaf," "Flowers," "Stem," "Root," and "Moss" are erasure poems that use text from John Ruskin's *Prosperina: studies of wayside flowers while the air is yet pure among the Alps and in the Scotland and England which my father knew, Volume I* (1879), chapters X, "The Bark"; III, "The Leaf"; IV, "The Flower"; VIII, "The Stem"; II, "The Root"; and I, "Moss," respectively.

"Stones" is an embellished erasure poem that draws text from John Ruskin's *Deucalion: Collected Studies of the Lapse of Waves, and Life of Stones* (1879).

"Clouds" is an extreme erasure poem that uses text from John Ruskin's environmentalist lectures, "The Storm-Cloud of the Nineteenth Century," delivered at the London Institution on 4 and 11 February 1884, and subsequently published in his collected works. These lectures document Ruskin's observations of the effects of air pollution resulting from industrialization upon the colour of clouds, constant and close observations that he made over a forty-year period (1831–71).

"Lines Left" is an extreme and partly imagined erasure poem based on my reading of Ruskin's *Love's Meinie: Three Lectures on Greek and English Birds* (1881), in particular, chapter III, "The Dabchicks."

"First and last stanzas from poems found in *The Worm's Kitchen* … " are emulations of the affect and logic of Edward Lear's *Book of Nonsense* (1846) and *Nonsense Songs, Stories, Botany and Alphabets* (1871), as well as Lewis Carroll's *The Hunting of the Snark* (1876). Each line of ellipses represents a missing stanza.

"Why I Am Not a Modernist" is a Mad Libs-style cut and replace redo of Frank O'Hara's poem, "Why I Am Not a Painter."

"Telempathus" is a reboot of Alfred Tennyson's "Ulysses" (1833/1842), spoken of an alternative version of Odysseus's son Telemachus, figured here as an insomniac empathy-artist.

"Two Limericks" are emulations of the kinds of poems found in Edward Lear's *Book of Nonsense* (1846) and the many other vocation- and labour-specific Victorian limerick poems found in Gershon Legman's extensive anthology, *The Limerick* (1991).

"Queen Victoria" was found by extraction in Leonard Cohen's song of the same title (found on *Live Songs*, 1973).

"Animal Slippers" is influenced by S.T. Coleridge's "The Rime of the Ancient Mariner. In Seven Parts" (1817 version), and Jerome McGann's article, "The Meaning of the Ancient Mariner," *Critical Inquiry* 8 (1981): 35-67. Early parts of the poem are inspired by passages from the Old Testament. The latter parts of the poem are inspired by the brilliant dialogues published in Oscar Wilde's *Intentions*, and by his *Complete Letters*, especially his long letter written between January and March 1897 during his last months in Reading Gaol, later published in a heavily edited text by Robert Ross under the title, *De Profundis* (1905).

"The Worms of Saint Peter's" is the one poem to have escaped in complete form from *The Worm's Kitchen*.

"Fudge in Entropy" is a dramatic monologue inspired by many examples of this Victorian form as it was perfected by Robert Browning, among them, "Johannes Agricola in Meditation" (1836). It is dedicated to the memory of Fudge and Blaze Camlot.

"Living Devices" is an imagined erasure poem based on the ongoing hum of John Ruskin's late madness in my ears.

Versions of some of the poems in *Vlarf* have appeared previously in the following places:

"Lost Days," "Mr Hyde at Home (The Musical)," "A Sonnet," "In the Criminal's Cabinet, Sherlock Holmes Discovers Himself," "Romantic Behaviour," "Men of Letters," "The Worms of Saint Peter's," and "The Fruit Man": *The Fruit Man and Other Poems* [limited edition poetry chapbook, with artwork by J.R. Carpenter]. Montreal: WithWords Press, January 2008. Thanks to Sasha Manoli and Ann Ward for making this lovely chapbook, with accompanying limerick bookmark.

"Flowers," "Genealogy," "Leaf," "Moss," "Root," "Stem," and "Stones": *Lines Crossed Out* [limited edition poetry chapbook, with artwork by Betty Goodwin] Montreal: Delirium Press, 2005. Thanks to Kate Hall and Heather Jessup for making *this* lovely chapbook.

"Lost Days": *Parliamentary Poet Laureate – Poet of the Week*. Selected by John Steffler. October 2007. https://lop. parl.ca/About/Parliament/Poet/poem-selected-former-poet-laureate3-e.html.

"Genealogy," "Birds," "Romantic Behaviour," "The Leaf," "In the Criminal's Cabinet," "Flowers," and "Stones": *Latchkey*. June 2006. n.p.

"In the Criminal's Cabinet": *In The Criminal's Cabinet: An Nthology of Poetry and Fiction*. London, England: Nthposition Press, 2004, 27.

"Leaves," "Stems," and "Flowers": *The Cyclops Review* Winnipeg: Cyclops Press, 2002, 77–83.

"In the Criminal's Cabinet Holmes Discovers Himself," "Men of Letters," and "Mr Hyde at Home (The Musical)": *Nthposition. com*. May 2002, n.p.

"Genealogy": *Journal of Literature & Aesthetics,* Kottam, Kerala, India (July-December 2001), 224–5.

I would like to thank my fellow NAVSA, BAVSA, AVSA, VSAWC, and VSAO Victorianists, bricky thinkers and kindly folks, all. (And thanks to my MSA friends, too.)

Sincere thanks to Allan Hepburn and Carolyn Smart for their generous support of this book, and for their keen editorial suggestions.

Heartfelt thanks to John Emil Vincent, ideal reader of *Vlarf* in its late manifestations.

Thanks with love to Cory, Oscar, Nava, Haika, and Finnick, my inspirations.